Contents

Words in **bold** can be found in the glossary on page 28

What is a city home?

A city is a place where thousands, sometimes millions, of people live and work. There are lots of buildings in a city, including offices, shops, factories and homes.

▼ About six million people live in the city of Rio de Janeiro in South America.

City homes

Nicola Barber

WAYLAND

First published in Great Britain in 2006 by Wayland,
an imprint of Hachette Children's Books

Copyright © 2006 Wayland

Hachette Children's Books
338 Euston Road, London NW1 3BH

Editor: Hayley Leach
Senior Design Manager: Rosamund Saunders
Designer: Elaine Wilkinson
Geography consultant: Ruth Jenkins

Printed and bound in China

British Library Cataloguing in Publication Data
Barber, Nicola
    City home. - (Homes around the world)
    1.Dwellings - Juvenile literature 2.City and town life -
    Juvenile literature
    I.Title
    643.1'091732

ISBN-10: 0-7502-4875-0
ISBN-13: 978-0-7502-4875-4

Cover photograph: townhouses and skyscrapers
in San Francisco, in the United States of America.

Photo credits: Andrew Holt/Alamy 6, Mark E.
Gibson/Corbis cover and 7, Mooch Images/Alamy
title page and 8, Felix St Clair Renard/Getty 9, Paul
Cchesley/Getty 10 and 27, Janine Wiedel
Photolibrary/Alamy 11, Yann Layma/Getty 12, Jane
Sweeney/Lonely Planet Images 13 and 26, Robert van
der Hilst/Corbis 14, Arcaid/Alamy 15, Michele
Falzone/Alamy 16, Demetrio Carrasco/Getty 17, Vincent
Laforet/Pool/Reuters/Corbis 18, Ulana Switucha/Alamy
19, Richard Levine/Alamy 20, Bill Bachman/Alamy 21,
Wendy Chan/Getty 22, Alex Segre/Alamy 23, John
Stark/Alamy 24, John Henry Claude Wilson/Getty 25.

Cities can be very crowded places. Some people live in large houses. Many people live in tall buildings that contain lots of homes. These are called flats or **apartments**.

◀ These houses are in San Francisco in the United States. There are office buildings in the distance.

City life
The world's tallest building is in the city of Taipei in Taiwan. It is 509 metres high!

Terraces and suburbs

In some cities, the streets are lined with houses that are all joined together in a long line. These are called **terraced** houses, or **townhouses**.

▼ *Rows of townhouses line the edge of the River Seine in Paris, France.*

Many people have their homes outside the city centre in areas called **suburbs**. The suburbs often lie many kilometres from the city centre. But they are still part of the city.

▲ These houses are in the suburbs of Stockholm, the capital city of Sweden.

Shanty towns

Across the world, people are moving from their homes in the countryside to live in big cities. It is often easier to find work in a city than in the country. People may not have enough money for a home in the city, so they build **shelters** in **shanty towns**.

▼ *People in this shanty town have built their homes from wood and* **corrugated iron** *in Ho Chi Minh City, Vietnam.*

Some city people do not have homes. They live on the city streets. They make shelters from bits of cardboard and plastic. There are homeless people in big cities all around the world.

▲ This woman lives in a shelter on the streets of London in England.

Building a city home

Many city people live in apartment blocks. These tall towers are made from **steel, concrete** and glass. Builders use the steel to make a strong **frame** for the building. They use the concrete and glass to make the walls and windows.

▼ People have no gardens in these apartments in Wuhan in China. Their **balconies** are the only outside space.

In other places, city homes are built using **materials** found nearby, such as mud or stone. People mix the mud with straw to make the building stonger.

▲ Many of the mud houses in Kano, Nigeria, have decorations on their roofs.

Inside a city home

Many cities are expensive and crowded places to live and lots of people cannot afford large homes. Families often live in small apartments. People may live, eat and sleep in just one or two rooms.

▼ *This woman lives in a small apartment in Shanghai, China.*

To find more space to live in, people have **converted** old buildings into homes. Many of these buildings were once **warehouses**, or offices. Now they are full of apartments.

15

The weather

In very hot places, people try to keep their city homes cool. In some cities, buildings have wind catchers on top. These wind catchers are like wide chimneys facing towards the wind. They trap the wind and the air goes into the rooms below.

▼ The city of Yazd in Iran lies in the middle of a hot desert. Wind catchers help to cool its houses.

It can get very cold during the winter in some cities. Moscow in Russia has snow on its streets in winter. Hot water is pumped through pipes to keep homes warm. People turn on electric radiators when the temperature drops very low.

City life

In 2006, the temperature went as low as minus 38° centigrade in Moscow.

▲ Winter in Moscow is so cold that canals and rivers freeze over.

The environment

A storm or **earthquake** can cause a lot of damage in cities because there are lots of buildings. In 2005, a **hurricane** hit the city of New Orleans in the United States. A hurricane is a big storm with strong winds and lots of rain.

▼ After a hurricane in New Orleans, **floods** from the River Mississippi filled homes and streets with water.

Often, the air in cities is not very clean. Smoke from factories and **exhaust fumes** from **vehicles** make the air dirty. Sometimes a city is covered with a cloud of air **pollution**, called **smog**.

City life

In 1995, an earthquake in Kobe in Japan killed more than six thousand people.

▲ In this picture you can see smog lying over the **skyscrapers** of Hong Kong.

School and play

City schools can be véry big, with hundreds of pupils. Some children may have come to the city from other countries. Many different languages may be spoken in one school.

▼ These girls are using computers as part of their school lesson in New York in the United States.

There are lots of different things to do in a city. Children can visit parks and city zoos. There are theatres and cinemas for going to see plays and films. There are libraries for reading books. There are swimming pools and places for playing sport.

▲ Actors perform a play outdoors in a park in Melbourne, Australia.

Going to work

City centres often have tall buildings, called skyscrapers, which are full of offices. Some people work in factories to make things, or they might work on the city's buses and trains.

▼ *Thousands of people go to work in these skyscrapers in Singapore.*

In city centres, people work in big **department stores** as well as small shops. People love to come to the city to go shopping. When they are not at work, many people go to the theatres and restaurants in the city.

City life
Macy's in New York is the largest department store in the world.

▲ Galeries Lafayette is a department store in the centre of Paris in France.

Getting about

There are lots of different ways to travel around a city. You can catch a bus, or go on a train. Some cities have trains that go through tunnels underground. Other cities have **trams** that run on rails in the streets.

▼ *People get on and off an underground train in Hamburg in Germany.*

Lots of people drive cars in cities. City streets are often full of cars. Sometimes the cars go so slowly that it takes a long time to go even a short distance.

▲ Cars and other vehicles are stuck in a long traffic jam on this street in Kolkata, India.

Where in the world?

Some of the places talked about in this book have been labelled here.

Look at these two pictures carefully.

- How are the homes different from each other?

- What is each home made of?

- Look at their walls, roofs, windows and doors.

- How are these homes different from where you live?

- How are they the same?

Kano, Nigeria

NORTH
AMERICA

San Francisco•

•New York

New Orleans•

ATLANTIC
OCEAN

SOUTH
AMERICA

PACIFIC
OCEAN

• Rio de Janei

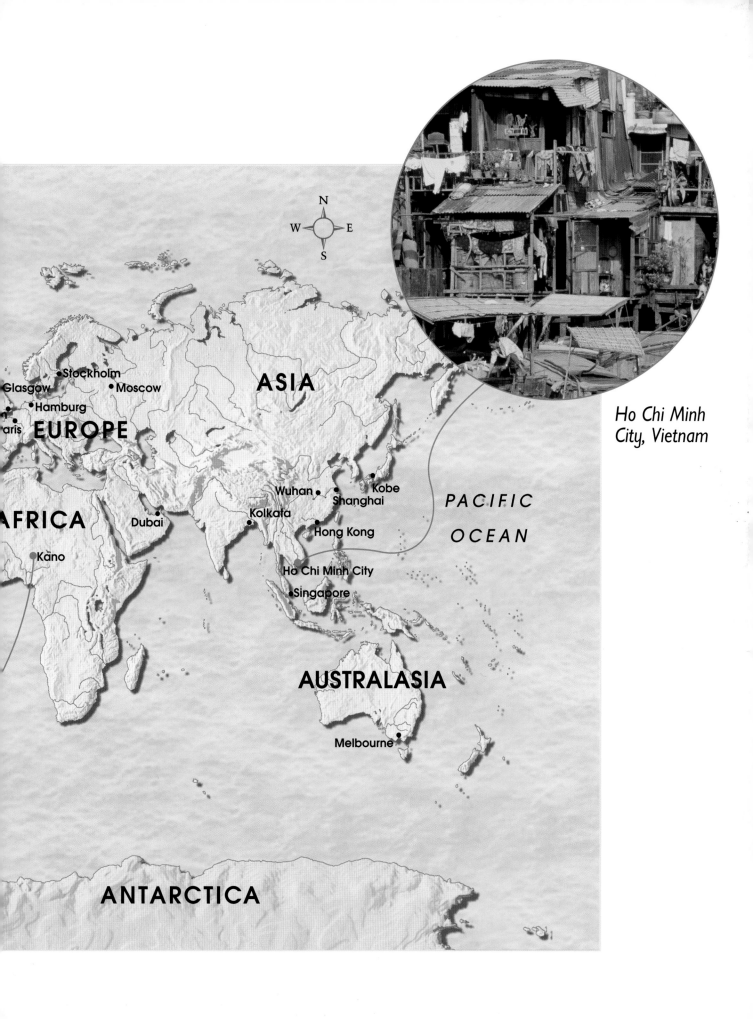

N
W · E
S

EUROPE

ASIA

PACIFIC

OCEAN

Stockholm
Glasgow
Moscow
Hamburg
Paris
EUROPE

AFRICA

Kano

Dubai

Kolkata

Wuhan
Shanghai
Kobe

Hong Kong

Ho Chi Minh City

Singapore

AUSTRALASIA

Melbourne

ANTARCTICA

Ho Chi Minh
City, Vietnam

Glossary

apartment	a set of rooms to live in, usually on one floor of a building
balcony	a small platform with rails that sticks out of a building
concrete	a mixture of cement, sand and water that is hard when dry
convert	to change into something else
corrugated iron	a sheet of iron that has ridges running along it
department store	a large shop with many different sections
earthquake	when the earth moves and shakes
exhaust fumes	waste gas that comes from the engine of a vehicle
flood	when water goes on to land that is normally dry
frame	a structure that gives something shape and strength
hurricane	a storm with strong winds and lots of rain
material	what something is made of
pollution	something that is dirty and dangerous to people
shanty town	an area of roughly built homes
shelter	any structure that provides some cover from the weather
skyscraper	a very tall building
smog	dirty air
steel	a kind of metal that is very strong
suburb	an area of homes on the edge of a city
terraced	describes houses that are joined together in a long line
townhouse	a house that is joined to its neighbours
tram	a kind of train that runs on rails set into the street
vehicle	any kind of transport with wheels, such as a car or a truck
warehouse	a large building used to store goods

Further information

Books to read

Starters: Homes Rosie McCormick, Wayland (2003)

We Come From India David Cumming Hodder Wayland (1999)

We Come From China Julia Waterlow Hodder Wayland (1999)

One World: In the City V. Guin, Franklin Watts (2004)

Where People Live: Living in Cities N. Morris, Franklin Watts (2004)

Websites

http://www.un.org/cyberschoolbus/habitat/index.asp
United Nations CyberSchoolBus website about cities

http://www.bbc.co.uk/schools/twocities/
Compare Belfast and Mexico City online

Index

All the numbers in **bold** refer to photographs.

A
apartments 7, 12, **12**, 14, **14**, 15, **15**

B
balconies 12, **12**
buses 22, 24

C
cars 25, **25**
cinemas 21
countryside 10

D
department stores 23, **23**

F
factories 6, 19, 22
flats 7

G
gardens 12, **12**

H
homeless people 11, **11**

M
mud houses 13, **13**, 26, **26**

O
offices 6, 7, **7**, 15, 22

P
parks 21, **21**

R
restaurants 23

S
schools 20, **20**
shanty towns 10, **10**, 27, **27**
shelters 10, 11, **11**
shops 6, 23
skyscrapers 19, 22, **22**
sport 21

steel 12
suburbs 9, **9**
swimming pools 21

T
terraces 8, **8**
theatres 21, 23
townhouses 8, **8**
traffic jams 25, **25**
trains 22, 24, **24**
trams 24

U
underground 24

W
walls 12, 26
warehouses 15
wind catchers 16, **16**
windows 12, 26
winter 17

Z
zoos 21

30